001870

BRIEF
FUNERAL
MEDITATIONS

BRIEF
FUNERAL
MEDITATIONS

Charles M. Chakour

ABINGDON PRESS
Nashville   Ⓢ   New York

BRIEF FUNERAL MEDITATIONS

Copyright © 1971 by Abingdon Press

ISBN 0-687-03980-0

Library of Congress Catalog Card Number: 70-134246

Scripture quotations noted RSV are from the Re-
vised Standard Version of the Bible, copyrighted
1946 and 1952 by the Division of Christian Education, National Council of Churches and are used by
permission.

SET UP, PRINTED, AND BOUND BY
THE PARTHENON PRESS, AT NASHVILLE,
TENNESSEE, UNITED STATES OF AMERICA

To Genevieve and

Cathy

Debby

and

Jim

PREFACE

The Christian ritual is a distinctive element of the Christian faith. Unlike the cultural practices of other peoples, the Christian ritual is not simply a sociological rite associated with life.

While other societies practice rites for birth and rites for death and the rites for the change of the season, the Christian faith has but one rite: the work of the people. This is simply to affirm the Word of God by giving assent to it. This is true for baptism, confirmation, communion, marriage, ordination, extreme unction, and all other sacraments or sacramental functions. It is also true of the Christian funeral.

It is true that the funeral customs of our Western culture in general, and our own country in particular, have been contaminated by accretions arising out of a blending of cultures and by the distinctive American penchant for pragmatic concerns as opposed to theoretic considerations. Nevertheless, the Christian funeral remains, and it becomes the burden of every clergyman to uplift it in order that the Word of God may be clearly affirmed and that the witnessing community may be empowered to give assent to it.

7

What this means in practical terms is that while the clergyman will operate in the given situation of the American funeral as it exists today, he will remember his teaching ministry is a tool which can keep both the mourners and himself free from its limitations. Likewise, while he will seek to comfort the bereaved (which is one aim of the whole funeral service), comfort will always be seen as stemming from the Word of God—the presentation of which is the clergyman's primary task. Coupled with the written word as found in the Scriptures, the spoken word of the pastor constitutes a powerful vehicle to achieve this end.

The meditations included in this book are written from this perspective. Far too often the homily is judged from the merit of its comfort value alone, and this comfort is usually seen as limited to consolation. Defined thus, anything which will bring even momentary consolation is considered fitting. But the Christian comfort is more than consolation. It is hope and strength and assurance founded firmly in faith. It is not so much man-centered as it is centered in God, who is the source of all comfort.

To make this point very clear, these meditations include no poetry. I have attempted to present the Word of God in clear relief with nothing to contend with it. Of course, while nothing can really contend with the Word of God, it is possible to blunt it and to throw it out of focus. Sometimes, for example, a "pretty" poem can distract from the beauty of the gospel.

I do not mean by this that poetry has no place in the Christian funeral, but for my purposes (and because this could not be an exhaustive compilation of poetry) I felt it was better to reserve the right to select suitable poems for the clergyman who finds poetry to be of real value and who knows how to use it well.

Illustrative material, too, is used sparingly in this book. This arises from design and out of theoretical considerations, not from a lack of desire for personal warmth or meaningful life situations to which the congregation can relate.

The homilies here are meant to be brief. Most illustrative materials would extend the length of the meditation beyond the time limits I feel would be wise. When such illustrations are employed they should seek to make a simple point and be brief enough that they do not approach the realm of "storytelling."

A further consideration in my selection of illustrative material is that it merge with the primary task of speaking the Word of God. What better place to seek such an example than from the lives of the saints and the classic stories of the faith?

I offer these meditations not as ends in themselves but as models for the design of what a Christian homily at a Christian funeral might be. To make this more explicit I include before each homily a statement as to the many considerations involved—the psychological, sociological, and the philosophical, as well as the demands of good grief therapy—which can aid in presenting the Word of God so that it can best be heard.

CONTENTS

SUDDEN DEATH

When death comes suddenly, the tragedy is that we focus on the death itself and the thought of dying because they are so suddenly thrust upon us that they obliterate the eternal question of life—life itself!

When the witnessing community gathers in grief, the comfort of their witness fails and is negated when their hearts and minds are fixed on the death itself and the suddenness of its coming. The clergyman must help the grief-stricken to turn away from the fact of the death in their search for comfort. They must turn to life and to the God of life. It is here and here alone that they may find solace and meaning.

The Meditation

> I wait for the Lord, my soul doth wait,
> and in his word do I hope.—Psalm 130:5

Death has come to our brother suddenly and as a thief. It was not looked for, nor was it expected. Not that death is ever easy or can ever be welcome, but coming like this—so quickly and so suddenly as to take us unaware—it brings with its pain an added dimension of shock and disbelief.

We cannot really accept the fact that one who so short a while ago was with us fully, sharing our life as we shared his, is now gone. It is difficult to believe that one

13

whose life was so full and so free could now be ended. How can we make our peace with the fact of death, coming as it does in the midst of our hopes still being hoped and our dreams still being dreamed?

Death will come—we know this—and while we are never fully prepared for it, we live with the reality of death as an ever-present fact of life. We have been told that a man begins to die the moment he is born. And so death is not the question. It is never the real question of life. God has not promised man that he will not die.

The question is not, "Shall we die?" or "How shall we die?" or "When shall we die?" or "Where?" but rather, "How shall we live?"

Life itself is the great question, and how we live it is ever before us.

To this question our brother has given his answer. We have known him and loved him and shared his life with him. He has lived fully and completely and well. Life was for him—as it is for all of us—hard, at times, and difficult. The questions of life are many and varied, and dealing with them is not easy. We succeed and we fail; we win a victory and we lose. But still we persevere. Amidst love and joy, mingled with grief and sorrow, we continue on our journey as best we are able.

So, too, has this our brother lived—as a man amongst men. Standing straight and tall and sure he has demonstrated that man is a noble architecture—more than just an intricate design of nerves and sinews.

Loving and being loved, sharing and serving, working and planning and hoping and dreaming, he lived his life amongst us. And he has won his battles and won his victories. Our tears attest to that.

Our lives have met and they have touched. The emptiness we feel at his departure is witness to this.

And what more can we ask? So much more can we desire, of course, and this desire will always move men to fight the great battles of life. But these desires are of time, they are not of quality. A life rich and well-lived is its own reward—a great victory unto itself, its own fulfillment.

Shall we seek not to die? No, this cannot be our goal! Will life have more meaning and purpose if we can but control how we die and when and where? No, for it is not the ending of life that gives that life its meaning and purpose. It is in the living of life that we must seek its purpose. It is in the living of life that even death finds its meaning. So it has been with our brother.

When Andrew, one of the apostles, was about to die a martyr's death nailed on the cross, he spoke words of comfort to those who were gathered at the place of his crucifixion and who were crying out against such punishment. He told them, while his hands and feet were bound to the cross, that even though his body was now held by death yet was he free in spirit, "for so it is appointed to depart out of the body and to be present with the Lord."

And turning to the proconsul who had ordered his death, Andrew spoke again of his spirit thriving free in the Lord, and he loudly affirmed that "he whom the Lord sets free cannot be bound, even by death, but is loosed by Jesus who himself was bound in death and yet lives free."

Witnessing his faith that while his body might die hanging upon the cross, his spirit would live by the grace of God, the blessed Andrew died while all who were present wept and lamented at their parting from him.

Such faith as this does not, of course, make death any

easier. But neither should the "how" of the death make the loss any more real. Death, in taking that which is most valuable—life—does its worst at any time and in any place.

So we will grieve at the coming of death, but we will grieve that life is gone. We will grieve that life is taken and that our brother is no longer with us. In so doing, however, we will be focusing on life and living—not on death.

The great questions of life will banish the questions of death, and we will move away from asking in this sad hour, "How shall a man die?" to "How shall a man live?" To this question let us give our answer in faith, as the Christ who lived for us and died for us has given us his answer.

DEATH OF A CHILD OR YOUTH

There is little a pastor can do in the most awful of hours, when a child is lost. In this day and age we are no longer prepared as were our parents for the possible loss of a child. We believe our children will one day mourn us, and not we them. Because of the advances of medical science, we are left defenseless in how to deal with such a loss. We have no psychological defenses which stand at the ready to come to our aid. The pastor has little experience in ministering at such a time, and friends are usually so griefstricken as to render them of little aid.

Yet the Church does have a word at this time, and it must be spoken clearly and without hesitation.

First, the pastor will simply assure the family that they are enveloped in the love of all who mourn with them. The simple fact of loving arms reaching out to them as they traverse the valley of the shadow demonstrates that they are not utterly alone and that others bear their burden with them.

But we are only men, and many men can grieve almost as much together as one man can grieve alone. We need God at this hour as he may not have ever been needed before. He is ready! The whole of our faith demonstrates from its inception that he is ready. He not only reaches out with loving arms as his children walk through the valley of the shadow, but he walks with them—for he has walked before. He is a father who has also lost a son!

The Meditation

> And [he] said unto them, suffer little children to come unto me, and forbid them not: for of such is the kingdom of God.
> —Mark 10:14

> He that spared not his own Son, but delivered him up for us all, how shall he not with him also freely give us all things?
> —Romans 8:32

Suddenly, in the fullness of youth, death has come. And it has brought with it the end of our dreams and hopes for this young life. This our child is dead, and so much of each of us has died with him.

What is it this pastor can say? What can any of us say to soothe and to calm or assuage the anguish of this moment? The grief of all is one—a grief that is shared. What can be said that will deny it? There is nothing! Death has come, and our grief in the face of it is great.

What can this pastor do at this moment? What can any of us do to make undone that which has come upon us? We know that anything we can do must fall short of that which we have hoped and prayed for.

We have prayed for life, but that is gone. And it seems our prayers are stilled before this awful act. We have prayed for help, yet it seems that it is far off. The only real help we seek at this moment is far from us and cannot pass the barrier of death.

We grieve. And well we grieve, for he who was precious

18

to us is gone. In the flower of his youth, still seeing visions, dreaming dreams and planning plans, he has been felled.

Our tears come. And how they flow for this child. They come hard from a fountain of pain, flowing through sorrow and from the innermost part of our saddened soul.

Today we cannot believe that we shall see the death of our children. In this day and age our youth are not taken from us. Medical science has all but promised us that our children will not die. It was our parents before us who lived with death. They lost their young ones in pestilence and plague and to fever and diseases. But we have been trained to believe that those days are no more. Little do we anticipate that we shall weep for our children in death. Rather, it appears that in this day and age, they will weep for us.

But today, all that is gone. Here in the presence of death, this family grieves this grief. And we too grieve with them.

We would have you know, dear family, that your sorrow is not yours alone. This outpouring of love which you have witnessed these past days testifies that a loss such as this belongs to the whole family of God—and that we are at one with you in this hour.

But what of God? How can it be, we ask over and over, that God seems so silent at this time?

His "still small voice," of course, we hear in our hearts. And many of us have sought to express what God must feel at this hour—love, comfort, mercy. We have expressed to each other that somehow God does know best, that though his ways are strange to us, yet he is wise. And we have said by way of comfort that God surely must have had a plan for this young life and a purpose now being fulfilled. As men of faith we can believe this. It is well to believe that he is "the author and finisher of the race that is set before us." And we do believe that as children of the household of God we must look to him for life's meaning.

But as men of faith we also look to him to act. It was his action in these days that we sorely have needed and have prayed for. Our hearts have cried out, "Where art thou, O Lord?"

Yet we cannot believe that he has removed himself from us. We cannot believe that he despises anything that he has made. We believe that he loves and cherishes his handiwork. Jesus said, "Let the children come to me, do not hinder them; for to such belongs the kingdom of God."

This same Jesus, the beloved son of God, both wept beside the grave and suffered death—even the untimely death of the cross.

Beloved, the Father has not promised that we will not die. The story of the Christian faith is the story of a son who died! The story of the Church is of a father who could not save his son from death.

It is in the light of this story that the death of this our child has its meaning—in faith. We have a father who knows of suffering and death. We have a father who has given up his own son—innocent and filled with youth!

And we have a faith that has proved the victory over suffering and death. Our Christ has shown that we shall not die forever—that death in God is swallowed up in victory!

We can be assured in this hour that he knows and that he understands. And we can believe that in our grief, we are made at one with the Father, for we can believe that in our loss he knows and he understands; his tears are mingled with ours.

20

DEATH OF A SERVICEMAN

The death of a serviceman is at once tragic and sudden and a great loss because of his youth. The sense of loss is complicated by the fact that such a tragic event happened after a long separation and at a great distance from the family home. The family is usually torn between ambivalent feelings of pride in the young man's service to his country and the meaninglessness of war.

The clergyman must support the family at an hour such as this by demonstrating to them that neither the life nor its loss is meaningless. He must be aware, however, that he not do this by extolling the virtues of military action as though it were sound Christian policy. This will not be the time for him to take any position on the war policy of the government or on war as an instrument of national policy; he must stand firmly in the theology of the Church, which asserts that God is the father of all men, and he grieves for the one who kills as he does for the one who is killed.

The Meditation

> Take your share of suffering as a good soldier
> of Christ Jesus.—II Timothy 2:3 (RSV)

Dear family, you have given up a son on the field of battle. You and he have paid a great price for all of us.

Our community and our nation has once again at great cost and sacrifice sent one of its own to war and has lost him. He is your child, but he is our child, too. You grieve, but we grieve too. You have lost him and we have lost him.

And it is at a time like this that we may well ask of God what part he has played. We seek, almost in vain, for some words of understanding and comfort as to why God should allow this to happen. But such understanding comes hard.

We know that God works for the best, and we believe this, but we are at a loss to understand how or why such a death can be for good. We know that God loved him and desired him, but we loved him and desired him, too. Life, at best, is short, and there was so much yet to share, to plan, to do.

We know that God is all wise, and we trust in his wisdom, but we fail to understand or to comprehend the wisdom which takes a young husband and leaves little children fatherless.

We cry to God for help and for understanding. We cry, "Why, O God, why?" We look to him for a reply, but no answer seems to come. We search the heavens, but the answer does not seem to be there. We search the Scriptures and we search our faith. We find comfort, yet we do not find understanding. And still we ask "why?"

The answers that we speak to ourselves do not suffice. It appears that neither the love of God, nor his wisdom, should mean the death of our loved one. The fault, if there is fault, cannot be placed at the foot of God.

Men die. We know this. Our living and our dying as men of faith are found in God. To believe this is commendable. To find the meaning of life and the meaning of death in our faith is to be a true child of the Father. But

22

this is not the same as finding God to be the cause of death. We must believe that God is the cause of life and is life himself. God must not, we believe, will the death of one so young. God, too, must have hoped and rejoiced at the thought of what this life could mean. We are sure that as Jesus wept beside the grave, so the Father weeps now at our loss.

If then, we cannot look to God for the answer, is it that we cannot look to God for any answer to this question of ours? Far be it! God, in Christ, has shown us where the answer is to be found. We must look to mankind. It is in man and in his relationship to others and to his God that we must first begin to seek understanding.

The Christ taught us that man was of supreme value in all the world. He taught us that man was most precious in the eyes of God, and that we ought to be precious to one another. He taught us to love God and to love one another.

But mankind has not learned this lesson. Our priorities are not yet the priorities of God. We persist in our separation—from one another and thus from God. Reconciliation is not yet the way of our lives—not as peoples, not as nations!

But we are beginning to learn. Amidst tears and sorrows at this hour, we ask again the questions of faith. We dedicate ourselves now to examining once again the life our Father would have us to live, so that less and less will a man be called upon to save the life of mankind by himself dying.

If the death of this young man in the service of his country moves us to commit ourselves to the high and noble causes for which he died, he shall not have died in vain. If liberty and freedom are nourished in our midst and if love and peace are now fervently sought after, then this death shall be considered even more glorious than its having happened in allegiance and service to one's nation. We shall see that it has become an instrument of God to move his people toward himself.

God once took a young man who had gone into the military service to protect his home and people against the hostile incursions of a neighboring enemy, and used him later as a faithful solider under the royal banner of Christ. We know this man as Ignatius Loyola. When he fell in battle, others took up the banner and fought that war while Loyola went on to a new battle—the battle of life which belongs to the kingdom of God.

Today others have taken up the banner of our fallen brother on that far-off field of battle. Let us take up his torch here at home, and let up keep faith with him. Let us dedicate ourselves that the kingdoms of this earth shall more and more reflect the kingdom of God.

A MEMORIAL SERVICE

The memorial service which is held several days after the private graveside services ought to be held in the church. The length of the service is usually longer than a funeral service, but should be much briefer than a Sunday morning worship hour. Congregational singing, a choir or soloist, and a homily are all very much a part of this service.

The theological consideration behind such a service is that the Christian community can and does continue to praise God in every facet of life—even at death. It recognizes of course, that the body has died, but it believes that life continues. To clearly lift up this faith so that we might focus on God and life (on things eternal and spiritual) rather than on man and death (on things temporal and physical), it is preferred that only family attend the body at its burial.

The community is then free to gather in faith for worship and praise. Such a service is seen as a memorial to what God has meant in the life of the deceased and in the life of all his children.

The memorial service is still a new phenomenon to many, and thus until a community has learned to accept the memorial service as such and can use it simply as a vehicle to deal with the more weighty matters of faith, every homily at such services will have the dual role of both fulfilling the nominal purposes of a funeral meditation and of assisting the worshipers to deal in faith with the novelty of the service itself.

One other caution must be observed. There will often be only one family member, and very few friends, who desire and who can fully appreciate such a memorial service. Others will "miss the body" and will thus "miss the funeral." This can be greatly overcome by the pastor if he will make several references to the deceased, and thus clearly allow the spiritual body to replace the physical. This is almost required by the exigency of the situation and is a magnificent teaching ministry.

The Memorial Service

The Organ Prelude

The Call to Worship:

> Lord, what is man, that thou hast regard
> for him?
> Or the son of man, that thou takest account
> of him?
> > Man is like a breath,
> > His days are as a fleeting shadow.
> > > —Psalm 144:3-4
> In the morning he flourishes and grows up
> like grass,
> In the evening he is cut down and withers.
> > —Psalm 90:6
> > So teach us to number our days,
> > That we may get us a heart of wisdom.
> > > —Psalm 90:12
> Mark the man of integrity, and behold the
> upright,

26

> For there is a future for the man of peace.
> —Psalm 37:37 (Hebrew version)

> Come, let us worship the Lord, Let us come before him in praise and in thanksgiving for the life which he has given us and for his love which sustains us.

The Hymn of Praise

The Scripture Lessons:

> So is it with the resurrection of the dead. What is sown is perishable, what is raised is imperishable.
> It is sown in dishonor, it is raised in glory. It is sown in weakness, it is raised in power.
> It is sown a physical body, it is raised a spiritual body. If there is a physical body, there is also a spiritual body.
> —I Corinthians 15:42-44 (RSV)

> (Also read selections from the Psalms, the prophets, the New Testament, or from the ritual of the church.)

The Anthem (choir or soloist)

Then shall the clergyman say:

> In this solemn hour, a memorial consecrated to our beloved dead, we reflect on the flight of time and the frailty and the uncertainties of life. We ask ourselves about the meaning of life: who are we, to what purpose is our wisdom and knowledge, and whence our strength and power? Our years seem few and frail and with much travail. But our

27

fathers have taught us to penetrate beneath appearances and to see deeper meanings, greater worth, and the real glory of human life as found in God. Such a view moves us from death to life and from hopelessness to hope.

A Prayer:

Our God and God of our fathers, in this hour which is sacred to the memory of yesterday and joyous in the faith for a tomorrow with thee, we thank thee for the blessings that have come to us through the love and devotion of————.

In this solemn hour, we recall his life and his faith as we recall other members of our congregation and families who have answered thy summons. They shall ever be remembered in the sanctuary of our hearts wherein we also remember thee and thy love for us. Amen.

A Hymn of Praise

The Meditation (A meditation is included following this outline)

A Prayer:

Father of mercies, in whose hand are the souls of the living and the dead, may thy consolation cheer us as we remember our beloved and honored dead who have gone to their eternal rest. May we be loyal to the memory of all our brethren, who in every generation sacrificed their lives to sanctify thy name. We beseech thee, O Lord, grant us strength to be faithful to their charge while the breath of life is within us. May their souls repose in peace and in the land of the living, beholding thy glory and delighting in thy goodness. Amen.[1]

A Hymn of Praise

The Benediction:

Magnified and sanctified be the name of God throughout the world which he has created according to his will. May his Kingdom be established in our hearts and may he who establishes peace in the heavens, grant peace unto us all. His name be blessed forever and ever. Amen[2]

The Meditation

Wherefore seeing we also are compassed about with so great a cloud of witnesses, let us lay aside every weight, and the sin which doth so easily beset us, and let us run with patience the race that is set before us.—Hebrews 12:1

In faith we gather at this hour a testimony to the life of our dear brother. He has lived well. He has lived a life befitting a child of God insofar as he was able. He loved

[1] From *The Sabbath and Festival Prayer Book,* by permission of the Rabbinical Assembly and the United Synagogue of America.
[2] Adapted from the Kaddish of the Jewish Service.

his Lord and he praised his name in the company of the saints. His words and his deeds were one, and found their meaning and purpose in God. He is a witness of the church to faith in action—a living, vital faith—healing, comforting, reconciling.

What can we add at this time? What can this pastor say or do to make more real his faith and his witness? What need he say? What need any of us say at this hour to bespeak the faith of he who lived so well amongst us as a brother in Christ?

There is nothing that can be said nor which must be said. His life has said it all: faith in God, love in Christ, service to man. He has radiated the love of God in his life and has coupled his witness to the witness of the fathers of the faith.

Amongst these is St. Anthony, who as a youth decided to live his life according to Christ's precept. He is, for us, the earliest known example of what becomes of one who fully obeys the demand of the gospel in all its implications. Overnight this rich young man became poor. Having given his wealth to the world, he prepared to give more: his life, in sacrificial service to others for the glory of God.

He had given all, when at the age of one hundred and five years he was finally taken away. After a life of service he found his final resting place; nobody knew where, for he wanted his body to belong to the earth and not to men. To them and for his God he had given his life in service and in faith.

Standing in such a tradition as this, our brother has run with patience the race that was set before him, looking to Jesus. There now remains for us to hear once again the testimony of faith and to reflect on it. In this hour, let the

30

Church speak to us again. Let the fathers of the Church, the psalmists and prophets through scripture, add their voices to his voice in death as he added his voice to theirs in life.

Let us hear once again the words of faith which he heard and which he believed: "I am the resurrection and the life, he who believes in me shall never die, and whoever lives and believes in me, though he die, yet shall he live." (John 11:25)

And what shall we add to this? Here we have faith expressed as he lived it. Here we have heard the psalmist and prophet speak again of life in God. And we have heard once again the Word of God coming to us in our Lord as he comforts us in love.

The testimony and the witness of the Church, and the fathers of the Church, coming to us in holy scriptures have reflected in death the testimony which he bore in life.

It remains for us, his brethren in faith—sisters and brothers of the household of God—to say to him: "May the angels take you into paradise: may the martyrs come to welcome you on your way, and lead you into the holy city Jerusalem. May the choir of angels welcome you and may you have everlasting life." [3]

[3] From the ritual of the Roman Catholic Church.

GRAVESIDE SERVICES ONLY

Often a pastor is called upon by a funeral director to officiate at graveside services. Most likely the deceased will be unknown to him and without a close family. In most cases the deceased will be aged or have lived alone for many years. He may also have resided in a distant community during his last years, and thus attendance at the graveside rites will be sparse.

The pastor must consider all of the above in planning his service. He will need to anticipate that the pallbearers, if there are any, will be virtual strangers to the deceased and to one another. Often such pallbearers are taken from the ranks of lodge members or other fraternal groups in which the deceased may long ago have been active. He will need to know that the request for graveside services was made to fulfill the minimum requirement for an honorable burial and that this carried with it the expectation that the service be brief.

The pastor can meet the demands of such a situation and yet remain true to his task by achieving a delicate balance between the two. He must not confuse the small group which gathers at the graveside with those who gather for the more customary formal service, and yet he must not seem to be encouraging the attitude that this is simply a duty to be dispensed with.

If the pastor recognizes that those who come are affirming something of the value of human life and are especially worthy of being ministered to, he can affirm the faith and help the small group gathered there to see itself as the image of the family of God. I believe that he can best do this by commencing the service in a very personal way. If he will address the group for a few brief moments before he enters upon the formal ritual of the church, he will help those present to become a true community (*koinonia*), and what might have been a simple perfunctory service will become an act of faith.

The Meditation

> Love one another with brotherly affection.
> —Romans 12:10*a* (RSV)

We gather at this grave, a small company. We are few in number and are, for the most part, strangers to one another. Yet we stand here together bound by a common concern and a common task.

We have come to lay to rest our brother and to gently entrust him into the hands of a waiting Father who loves him. But we have not come just because death has brought us. Death has no power to bring men together. While we gather in the presence of death, we come because of life, and we come to affirm the value and the reality of life.

It is because this brother lived amongst us, and laughed and wept as we do, that we gather here. We come, not because he died, but because he lived. We come not because we must, for there is nothing that compels us—any of us— to be here. Rather, we come to affirm that he is our brother and that we have shared life together.

33

As such, we are no longer strangers to one another, but in our coming we have become a community, a family: members one of another. What binds all men to each other binds us also, and we here affirm that this is true.

This ought to be especially clear to each of us, for in our few numbers, and stripped of all the numerous formal reasons why men gather at such a time as this, we can see the simple fact that we are our brother's brother and children of the one Father. It has been said that strangers are friends who have not yet met. The Christian faith accepts this, of course, but adds that these strangers are brothers.

In spirit, then, let us join together to express the faith of the church and hope in the promise of God.

THE AGED: SENILE, CRIPPLED, BEDFAST

Death comes so often as a thief that we fail to realize life can rob, too. When one of great age or who was long ill dies, there is often a feeling of great relief. Grief is absent and sorrow almost gone. And this is as it ought to be, of course, but most often it results not from the fact of a merciful death, but from the fact that the deceased has long since ceased to be seen as a person. Because old age and prolonged illness have already robbed this life, there is little left for death to take. The family has long since mourned this former loved one.

One can find no quarrel with this psychological manifestation, but despite it, and almost because of it, the personhood and humanity of the deceased need to be reaffirmed from the point of view of the One who is father of this life. Only when this is done does the family have restored to them a loved one who can be committed to God in faith and in trust.

The Meditation

> Lord, thou hast been our dwelling place in
> all generations. Before the mountains were
> brought forth, or ever thou hadst formed the

earth and the world, from everlasting to everlasting, thou art God.—Psalm 90:1-2

The hour of death has come. As we gather in the face
of death, we know that it has not come as a thief, but
almost as a friend. Death has brought peace and rest. But
we are filled with grief at its coming, for we cannot easily
give up or surrender one we love.

We grieve for our brother whom we have lost. And we
grieve for ourselves, for we loved him. Yet even in the
face of our sorrow, we confess that we would not wish him
back to a bed of pain.

And so death seems strange to us at this hour. While
our fear of it seems unfounded, yet we shudder in the face
of it. It has come as a friend, yet we dread its coming. It
has brought rest and peace, yet we would flee from it.

We are confused by the mingling of our fears and our
feelings. We find ourselves exclaiming, "O, God! " as we
contemplate what death means; yet hardly have we expressed our anguish when we find ourselves uttering a
simple "Thanks be to God" for his mercy.

And it is the later confession of faith that will in time
fully color the meaning of this hour to us. Of course, the
giving up of our brother will never be easy, and there will
long be tears, but the pain of it will be gone. And as the
immediacy of this death passes, we will see it more and
more as comfort and rest and peace.

And so death has not really taken our brother from us.
Rather, and in many ways, it has taken one who, through
age and pain, seemed lost to us, and restored him to us
again. Our hearts know this and our tears attest to it.

But while death has not taken him from us, as a thief

would take, it is possible that life can do this. If we look at our brother as he was in these later days alone—days of illness and suffering and of old age—we are in danger of measuring the whole of his life by its ending. In so doing, we permit life to rob him and to rob us of him and his total being.

But man is not just what his later days have become. The totality of his being is the fullness of the whole of his life. If we forget this, then we forget this our brother, and giving him up comes much too easy.

We must remember him as the person he was: that once he was young, and that he loved and was loved. We must recall that once he hoped hopes and dreamed dreams and planned plans. We must see him in his days of joy and happiness, laughing his laughs; and in days of sorrow and grief, shedding his tears. We must see him again in the days of his youth, a young man of honest toil, with vitality for life and living. And we must see him living as we all do, amidst the uncertainties of life, with its rewards, with its pains, and with its joys.

If we can see our brother again in this way—see him anew—then he will be restored to us, even in this hour of death.

Let us not permit life to do what death has shown it cannot do: take him from us. Let us remember that the measure of a man is the fullness of his life, and let us see that fullness restored in this hour.

Though our grief will continue, it will be a grief that is genuine and real: a sense of loss for one who loved and hoped and dreamed and is now gone.

And we can trust in God, who gives us life, and who gave him life, that the full meaning of that life is to be found in grace—the love of God. For it is this love that gives to man his meaning and his purpose and that makes the whole of life real and true. In this spirit we bid farewell to this our brother who is restored to us in Christ, where faith, hope, and love abide.

THE WITNESS OF A CHRISTIAN
FAMILY THROUGH A LONG ILLNESS

In this day and age, when the family is being challenged on every side, there is need for the Church to support it whenever the opportunity arises. What better time to do this than when the family comes into focus at the death of a member. At such a time it is possible to witness to the family as a unit, concerning its value in the life of its members, to draw strength and support for each member from the entire family as a family, and to witness to the family of God.

This is especially true when the family is Christian in the fullest sense of the word, and when it has worked as a family at its best. As such, it has not only appropriated for itself the value inherent in the Christian family, but has borne a witness to the community at large as to the meaning and worth of family life.

These points are often missed, however, in the face of death. The family is often worn and weary and, in the face of apparent failure, focuses on death rather than on life. The clergyman can be of great service here by pointing up these values and the real victory of life which this faithful family has won. By so doing, he can give this family new strength and dignity, while he also demonstrates its witness to members of other families who are present.

The Meditation

> Wherefore I desire that ye faint not at my tribulations for you, which is your glory. For this cause I bow my knees unto the father of our Lord Jesus Christ, of whom the whole family in heaven and earth is named.
> —Ephesians 3:13-15

The psalmist wrote of the valley of the shadow of death. We today know something of that dark valley. This our brother has been walking it for so long a time, and we who loved him have walked with him. The steps were slow, halting, painful. Both in his life and in ours, there have been other valleys, but the valley of the shadow of death is of a singular kind. Men are not prepared to walk it, nor to endure it. We cannot walk it alone.

And so it is a testimony to love and to life and to faith that you have journeyed into this valley to walk it with this brother. In family bonds and with bonds of friendship and brotherhood, you have been companions one to another as over the months the valley deepened and its gloom grew.

Hope, in the face of hopelessness. Joy, in the midst of sorrow. Life, in the midst of death. This comfort and peace was possible because, in love, you walked together.

Death itself holds no terror. It is the coming of death, the lonely journey through the valley, that is to be feared. But in love you have vanquished this fear.

Death is here, to be sure, and we know it has taken our brother from us. Its grief and sorrow are very much a part of our life. But more than death is present. Love is here. Hope is here. Life is here!

Love shines through the loneliness of death and abolishes

the loneliness. When we see it at work in this family and in this wide circle of friends, we know it is real. We see it now, and we have seen it over these past months. Family being real family. Church becoming real Church. Friends becoming like unto brothers. Love has made itself our companion in the midst of that valley!

Hope, too, is with us, even in the face of our hopelessness at this time. And our trust in God, as the psalmist trusted in him when he walked through that dark valley, sustains us.

And life is here—even as death is here. Our sorrow and our grief testify to the validity of life and to its value. Life well-lived and well-shared, as this life has been shared, shines so brightly and so well that it all but obliterates death. With the strength of such meaning, can death overcome?

And God is here. It is he who gives strength to pass through the valley of death. It is he who has called us to walk with this our brother in his journey. It is he who has been the great companion, "for thou art with me, thy rod and thy staff, they comfort me."

As he has walked with this our brother through the valley of death, so too will he walk with us as we continue in our journey of life. Just as he is the God of death, victor over it and turning it to his own meaning and purpose, so too is he the God of life, victor over it and turning it to his own will and purpose.

In the year A.D. 155 a bishop of the Church, Polycarp of Smyrna, was arrested and burned at the stake in a vast arena. What the authorities felt was surely an experience so taxing to the Church as to hasten its destruction was turned into a glorious victory by those who underwent the ordeal of suffering with the beloved Polycarp.

The proconsul urged him to save his own life out of respect for his great age, but Polycarp replied, "Eighty and six years have I served him and He hath done me no wrong, how then can I blaspheme my king who saved me?" Polycarp would not confess that his suffering had come at the hands of the Lord and would not, even though in great pain, deny him.

The multitude, seeing the faith of this man and of those who suffered with him, marveled at this testimony of faith and were led to the Lord.

And you have witnessed to this truth. Your sustaining love and faith have won the victory. You have brought victory in the face of the defeat which is death. You have demonstrated that in the midst of anguish and pain, in the midst of frustration and fear, and despite all weariness and sacrifice, love is able to win the victory, and faith to save the day.

The battle of life has been fought and won in this our brother. And you have won it with him. As you have won this victory, so too can you be assured that the victory lingers on. This strength and faith which here came to the fore is not given up and gone, but is revitalized, rekindled, and renewed.

Just as the Father has walked with us in these days of despair and death, so too can we believe that he will continue with us now. Just as he has won the victory over the loneliness of death—as is amply demonstrated in this family —so too can we be assured he will win the victory of life, giving strength in the days ahead.

A COMPLETE SERVICE WITHOUT
USE OF A FORMAL HOMILY

In the best tradition of the Church, no Christian service of any type is ever conducted without at least a brief homily, for the service is always a witness to the Word. In the funeral service, however, there is always much danger that this service may become a witness to the life of a person. It must never be so! At best, when the life of the deceased is brought into focus, it must always be the Christian concept of life that is fixed upon, and the meaning of that life in Christ.

Even here, however, there is a danger that the clergyman will border on eulogy and praise for the departed Christian rather than on praise of the God to whom his life pointed. The Roman Catholic Church had long forbidden such practice and the custom had been to have the same service for each person—all of whom are equal before God. With this heritage, there is little danger that Catholic clergy will commence canonization of the departed now that the homily is a part of every service.

Protestants, however, need a special discipline to assure that the word which is spoken is spoken in praise of God. The suggested service which follows is one attempt at such a practice. In the extended remarks of the pastor, the word is clearly heard while the personal character of the homily is retained.

The Service

Let the following passages of Scripture be read:

> Jesus said . . . , I am the resurrection, and the life: he that believeth in me, though he were dead, yet shall he live; and whosoever liveth and believeth in me shall never die.
> —John 11:25-26

> The eternal God is thy refuge, and underneath are the everlasting arms.—Deuteronomy 33:27*a*

> The Lord is my light and my salvation; whom shall I fear? The Lord is the strength of my life; of whom shall I be afraid?—Psalm 27:1

> For we know that if our earthly house of this tabernacle were dissolved, we have a building of God, an house not made with hands, eternal in the heavens.—II Corinthians 5:1

Let us pray:

> Here let the pastor offer a prayer affirming that God is our refuge and strength and help in time of trouble. Then let the prayer become a petition in which his help is sought, so that we may be enabled to put our trust in him at this and every time of need.

In the Old Testament there is a psalm, one we all know —Psalm 23—in which a man of faith facing an hour of sadness and loss and death turns to God. He speaks of the valley of the shadow in which his life now seems to be lost. He knows that death is his companion and that evil is present in the world. Life is hard and pressures are great, dreams turn to nightmares and hopes fade. Yet in faith he proclaims that he has hope, for walking with him through the valley of the shadow is his God. And though death be his companion, yet he knows in faith that since God walks with him also, his life here will have meaning and purpose, for he has found new life in God.

He cannot avoid that valley, but he is able to overcome it. And it is this victory of life and love and hope that causes him to proclaim, even while in the midst of the valley, that the Lord is his shepherd, that his soul is restored, and that he will dwell in the house of the Lord forever.

Hear this man of faith as he speaks to us today:

> The Lord is my shepherd; I shall not want.
> He maketh me to lie down in green pastures: he leadeth me beside the still waters.
> He restoreth my soul: he leadeth me in the paths of righteousness for his name's sake.
> Yea, though I walk through the valley of the shadow of death, I will fear no evil: for thou art with me; thy rod and thy staff they comfort me.
> Thou preparest a table before me in the presence of mine enemies: thou anointest my head with oil; my cup runneth over.
> Surely goodness and mercy shall follow

45

me all the days of my life: and I will dwell
in the house of the Lord forever.—Psalm 23

And again from the Old Testament, we read of one who
was filled with sorrow and grief. Help seemed far off.
Though he looked all about him, he could find no comfort.
Searching afar—even to the distant hills—offered no promise of peace. He cried out: "Where will my help come
from?" In faith, though, he found his answer. His help
came to him from God. It was in God that the meaning
and purpose of life were to be found. It was from God
that real peace was to be had. In joy, then, he exclaimed the
faith that our help is to be found in God, and that this
God is near to us, and that we are kept by him.

Hear this psalmist in his cry of pain as he bespeaks his
need and our need, but hear him also as he speaks of God,
in whom we find our help:

> I will lift up mine eyes unto the hills, from
> whence cometh my help.
>
> My help cometh from the Lord, who made
> heaven and earth.
>
> He will not suffer thy foot to be moved:
> he that keepeth thee will not slumber.
>
> Behold, he that keepeth Israel will neither
> slumber nor sleep.
>
> The Lord is thy keeper: The Lord is thy
> shade upon thy right hand.
>
> The Lord shall preserve thy going out
> and thy coming in from this time forth, and
> even for evermore.—Psalm 121

In the New Testament, we have the words of our Lord,
who, in the midst of death—even the death of the cross—

sought to bring comfort and peace to those around him.

Facing his own imminent crucifixion, he nonetheless thought, not of himself, but of those he loved. In seeking to comfort them and to give them strength to face life fully and unafraid, he told them of new life in God—and he shared his own hope and faith with them—speaking of life and truth and love.

In that moment of death, he turned the eyes of those who loved him to life and to hope. As he spoke to the Church in that day and at that time and at that place, so hear him as he speaks to his Church here and now—at this time and in this place:

> Let not your heart be troubled: ye believe in God, believe also in me. In my Father's house are many mansions: if it were not so, I would have told you. I go to prepare a place for you. And if I go and prepare a place for you, I will come again, and receive you unto myself; that where I am, there ye may be also. . . .
>
> I am the way, the truth, and the life. If ye love me, keep my commandments. And I will pray the Father, and he shall give you another Comforter, that he may abide with you for ever; even the Spirit of truth; whom the world cannot receive, because it seeth him not, neither knoweth him; but ye know him; for he dwelleth with you, and shall be in you.
>
> I will not leave you comfortless: I will come to you. Because I live, ye shall live also.

> Peace I leave with you, my peace I give
> unto you: not as the world giveth, give I
> unto you. Let not your heart be troubled,
> neither let it be afraid.
>
> —John 14:1-7, 15-17, 27

And again from the New Testament, we have the words of John, the last of the apostles, aged, frail of body and ill, in prison on the island of Patmos. He had seen the crucifixion of his Lord, the martyrdom of the apostles, and the persecution of the Church. His eyes had wept bitter tears for those he loved, his ears had heard their cry of pain, his voice had been raised almost constantly in prayer for the suffering Church. Now in great age and separated from those he loved and himself facing death, though his ears could hardly hear, he spoke of hearing wonderful things, and though his eyes could barely see, he spoke of seeing the glory of the Lord. Because of his faith and because he knew that God was with him, he was able, with a mouth that was feeble and frail, to speak of hearing the comforting words of God and of seeing the promise of God.

In the midst of trial and tribulation and suffering and death, he spoke to the grieving Church of his day, and he speaks to us here and now when he says:

> And I John saw the holy city, new Jerusalem,
> coming down from God out of heaven. . . .
> And I heard a great voice out of heaven
> saying, Behold, the tabernacle of God is with
> men, and he will dwell with them, and they
> shall be his people, and God himself shall
> be with them, and be their God.

And God shall wipe away all tears from their eyes; and there shall be no more death; neither sorrow, nor crying, neither shall there be any more pain; for the former things are passed away.—Revelation 21:2-4

Let us pray:

Here a suitable prayer may be offered in which the name of the deceased may be raised to God and the concern for family and friends be lifted up. This prayer should close with a benediction.

WHEN AN OBITUARY IS
INSISTED UPON

In many areas of our country today, the obituary is no longer considered a valid or necessary part of the funeral service. This derives from the ready availability of local news media through which a full obituary can be easily circulated. To read an obituary at the funeral service after it has been published or read on the air is unnecessary so far as the purpose of the Christian funeral is concerned. In our modern world, therefore, the obituary seems more and more to be a part of the secular culture, with the funeral service reserved exclusively for the greater religious concerns of faith, promise, and comfort.

Not only this, but the true nature of the funeral service is being restored from a memorial service in which the deceased is memorialized and eulogized to one of affirmation of the good news of Christ that in him is life. In such a service, the major element and the full thrust is directed at what God has to say to us through the fathers of the faith as they are heard by the Church through the Scriptures. An obituary seems strangely out of place in such a service.

Yet, if a funeral is anything, it is also tradition and custom. To many, an obituary is a required ingredient, a necessary custom and the only factor which is exclusively personal, and which thus can demonstrate just what this service is about.

The clergyman will, from time to time, face a situation where an obituary is already prepared and handed to him for use in the service. I believe that at such times the faithful pastor, ever alert to situations which will allow him to be teacher, can find in this occasion the possibility to use the awkward and humble tool which is the obituary for both teaching a gospel message and to bring comfort. The following is such an example:

The Meditation

So teach us to number our days that we may apply our hearts unto wisdom.—Psalm 90:12

(Upon completing the reading of the obituary, the clergyman may enter directly into the meditation.)

Here, then, before us is the life of our brother: dates, persons, places, events. All are important. But life is more than a series of dates and names and places. Each signifies some step along the way in which he mingled his life with others, was touched by those who loved him and whom he touched. Days of joy, the hour of pain—living, moving, breathing, planning—as he lived out his life.

This is what these dates mean: a day in which he was loved and tenderly held, a day he loved and entered into a holy relationship, a day in which he laughed for joy, and another in which he shed his tears in sorrow and grief.

And the places (name some from the obituary), these are more than cities and towns in the life of our brother. One he called his childhood home, where he played and laughed and learned and grew. Another is where he labored and took his part side by side with mankind in the earnest business of life and living.

And, of course, the names which are a part of his life—not just names but names of people—persons who gave him life and with whom his life and hopes and fears were shared. For each name there is a person who showed him his reason for being; one who cradled him in love and nurtured him; one with whom he shared a holy relationship. With these persons he laughed in life, and with some and for some he wept—and some weep here today.

The name of Augustine is familiar to us all, but the events of his life are not so well known. When one reads the biography of this great man, one finds hidden beneath the facts of that life the mystery and wonder it contains.

One can hear the date of his birth and the date of his death, and even of the places in which he lived—Numidia in the eastern part of the province; Rome; Milan; the whole of the Roman world—and still miss the life of this man. One can see life along the Nile River and the impressions that were visited upon a growing boy—worldly pursuits, business, and pleasure. And one can see that he looked upon education as synonymous with compulsion and punishment and regarded his lessons and studies as a painful torment. All of this we can see and still not know why Augustine is so loved.

But Augustine did become the scholar of the Church and one of its greatest saints. To learn why, one must know something of the saintly Christian who was his mother,

Monica. And one must hear her faith-inspired words as she spoke to her son concerning a long and tortuous vigil of devotion at the basilica—a demonstration of faith when the basilica was taken by storm. One must suffer with Augustine in his "delirium of grief" over the loss of a friend. One must see, too, how the great Bishop Ambrose moved in his life and completely opened it to the Lord.

Only when these are seen can Augustine be fully seen for the first time. So must Saul's encounter with Christ on the road to Damascus be seen before the new Paul who came out of that encounter be understood. So must young Anthony be seen in church, hearing the words of the pastor who ministered to him, before one can understand why he arose and went to give away all his possessions and to become a saint of God. In each of these, it is the hand of God touching life in many ways, at many times, in many places, and through many persons that made the difference.

And so we might ask, what is the measure of a man's life? Is it the day he was born and the day he dies? Is it a simple accumulation of events and places or of names and dates? It is not! We are measured by the timelessness of God's love. The fullness of our life is to be found in the meaning of new life in him. As we, in faith, die in him, so do we know that as we live, it is in him that we live and move and have our being.

It is through our God, as he comes to us in Christ, that we see the measure of our lives and who makes our lives full. It is he who gives meaning to the day of our birth, and to each of our days, as we partake in the full stream of life and living. It is he who blesses our relationship with other persons, and in whom the meaning of these relationships can be found. Thus, the whole life of a man is to be found in God. It is in him that our life finds meaning. At death, then, we do not find ourselves entering a new relationship or one which is so foreign or so strange to us. For as in life, we are found in God, and it is he who gives us our meaning. So too in death can we believe that even our dying is held in the hands of the Father—that he knows and that he cares.

As in faith those who loved our brother received him from the Lord at his birth, so too let us in faith give him up unto the Lord. For our life at its ending, as in its beginning and its living, is to be found in the heart of God.

THE HUMANISTIC FUNERAL

Paul E. Irion in his excellent book, *The Funeral—
Vestige or Value,* states "In all candor, we must acknow-
ledge that the religious elements of the funeral are not
meaningful to all. If the funeral is seen only as a religious
service, it either denies to the nonreligious person some of
the nonreligious values because he cannot participate in
its meanings, or it compels him to participate hypocritically
and therefore without meaning." [1]

Mr. Irion raises the question as to how the clergy can
serve at such a time and yet be true to the feelings, under-
standings, and needs of the mourners. He says that in order
to do this, the funeral will have to be modified as seen
from the Christian perspective. He does not feel, however,
that such modifications need destroy all the values of the
Christian funeral.

I agree. I feel that when I am called upon to officiate
at a humanistic funeral I ought to be as personal as possible
with the family—sharing its sense of loss and coming in
supportive aid as a person to persons in need. I do not deny
my faith, but I do not inflict it upon the family. My
subliminal hope, I would suppose, is that they will know
that part of my reason for coming is that the Church knows

[1] (Nashville: Abingdon Press, 1966), p. 189.

and cares about their loss. The service itself, then, can more easily reflect this, and the meditation can be seen in this light.

The Meditation

> What man is he that liveth, and shall not see death? shall he deliver his soul from the hand of the grave?—Psalm 89:48

> Man goeth forth unto his work and to his labour until the evening.—Psalm 104:23

We are creatures of the earth. It is in this world that we live and breathe and have our being. It is here where we mingle our lives and share in one another's joys and burdens.

Each man is called to his own time. We are called to this hour and to this place. Our day is today, the latter half of the twentieth century: the day of the atom and the day of space.

Each man throughout history has lived out his life in his own time. Each generation has come and gone in its own season. Yet neither man nor his generation lives in isolation from other men or from other generations. Each age is the dying of one dream and the birth of another.

We are, all of us, the children of yesterday and the heritage of those generations yet unborn. We stand in line upon that endless path trod by mankind. Whether that path be one of splendor or one of decay depends in large part upon each of us, each man who has ever lived.

We need to reflect upon this so that our life and its meaning may be seen in perspective. We live and we die, but as we do not live alone, so too is our death not one of isolation. Death is a part of our life, and marks, as does our birth, that portion of mankind's path which we have trod. As in birth we commence that portion of the journey which befalls us, so too at death do we complete it. The one must follow the other as surely as night follows day. But as the night is a part of the day, so too is death a part of life. We can accept this because we can understand it. And we can understand it because this is the way the world is made. It has ever been so!

At death, then, we are parted one from another. One man's journey is done. He has completed the race which is set before him; the journey of the other man continues. But where the two paths were joined, where life and love have been shared, history will ever record that these two have walked together. As in their hearts they shared that pathway of life, so after death do those who remain remember that shared journey.

And so death, while in many ways very real, is not so final as to utterly obliterate the meaning of one's life. It is natural, universal, and impersonal, of course, but since it is a part of life, it cannot be understood outside of life itself.

The question of life is not one of death, but of life itself: how shall we live and walk among men?

The day in which we live is the day allotted to us. We must focus on that. We must seek to find meaning and purpose in our lives, so that while we live, we live fully, and when we die, we are not truly lost. For that part of us which gave meaning and purpose to our life continues in the memories and the lives of those about us.

Man is an intricate design of nerves and sinews, but

he is more. In the fullness of his life he is touched not only by the lives of those with whom he lives, but by the lives of those who have passed his way before. With his life he also touches those yet to come. It is this that gives our lives meaning and sets us apart from the rest of creation. It is this that causes the world to take note of our coming and to pause at our passing.

We start our race, we set our mark, we complete our course. This is life! That we have lived is a part of the record of man. How we live is the choice each of us must make.

Committal

As we are a part of all mankind, mingling our lives with one another, so too are we a part of nature. It is of the stuff of the earth that we are made. We live for a while; we breathe and have our being as we walk upon the earth. But in all of this we are a part of the totality of creation from which we have been made, and amongst which we live as persons. We are men, to be sure, seeking ever higher ground, and searching whereby we may partake in the order and design of the world order; but we are natural men too, and in death we recognize this once again. Our testimony here at this graveside is that, while out of this earth has sprung a life with meaning and value, it remains ever a part of the earth which gave it birth.

We return the body itself to the earth, for it is from nature that it has sprung and to which it has always belonged; but the meaning of that life we claim for ourselves, for it was in our shared lives that this meaning is now to be found.

THE NONBAPTIZED PERSON

Often the clergyman will be called upon by church members to officiate at services for a deceased relative who has never been baptized. The concerned Christian will be anxious for some assurance, and will most likely be confused in his own emotions of love and respect for the "good life" of this loved one and his understanding of the teachings of the Church in this regard.

Of course, every pastor will be bound both by his own theological perspective and that of his church, but even within these limits he ought to be able to demonstrate the love of God as understood in the concept of grace as the unearned, undeserved, free love of God.

The Meditation

> Therefore being justified by faith, we have peace with God through our Lord Jesus Christ.—Romans 5:1

What is it that man is able to claim? Life? Surely not. For it is given to us for but a season. Wealth? It decays before our eyes and is gone. Our body? It soon grows old and dies. All that we have and all that we are in this earthly life is but a temporary possession.

In life, one man has much of one thing, another has little. One seems blessed with much comfort, with good health, or with great success; another lacks all of these. All men come equally to death, however, and death fully claims each of us. Death is no respecter of persons, and at death the poor man and the rich man—the peasant and the king are seen as equal.

But it is not death that causes us to be equal. Death has no such power. In the eyes of God, and in his heart, all men are equal indeed. Each of us is summoned before our Lord and each of us given an assigned task. We are each given our course to run. To each—the quiet Christian, you, me, the saints, the apostles, and this our deceased brother—the Lord gives the same charge, the same calling.

It is true, of course, that we vary greatly in our talents and ability, but when it comes to the real heart of the matter, wherein the meaning of life is to be found, God is the same father to one child as he is to another—each of us receives the same measure from his hand.

All of us—the great and the small, the sinner and the saint, the church member and the man in the street—come under the grace of God—his love. Such grace is best understood as that love of God with which he loves us though we have not earned it, are not worthy of it, and do not deserve it. It is his love coming to us because he wills to love us. God is not a respecter of persons and will not be mocked. He desires to love us on his own initiative, and he will not be thwarted in that love. He freely gives of himself. There are no conditions which must be met, no conditions which must be fulfilled.

God calls to each of us by name. We are precious to him. We are known! We are members of his household who are known and loved—not by any merit on our part, but on his part alone.

It is this which each of us can claim—this name we carry as a loved child of God, as one who is known. It is this and this alone which any of us and all of us have. We are loved!

As one who is loved, each of us can come to the Father, knowing that we are found worthy, believing that we will be received, and trusting that he has been waiting for us.

Our salvation, then, is not a matter of who we are or what we are, or who we have been or what we have been. It rests in the hand of God, who freely gives to us. We do believe this, but to take him seriously we must fully take him at his word, and trust that he will act in love the way he said he would act.

With this kind of faith, our life can have new meaning, as in life we commit ourselves to him. But this love is not merely a matter belonging to life; it belongs to God, who is able to overcome all barriers to visit his grace upon us.

When Ambrose was a political officer in his native city of Milan during the fourth century, he knew very little of the Church and cared less. But there arose a time when the Church faced a crisis of great magnitude, and Ambrose was called upon to settle the dispute and to bring peace to a newly restored Church. He was an outsider and sought by force of arms to resolve the issue. Little did he know at that time that God had resolved to settle upon him.

The Christians cried out for Ambrose to lead the Church to new high ground, and although Ambrose fought desperately against it, he could not successfully contend with God, who by his grace had selected him. In the space of a week, Ambrose was on his way to become the "father of the Church." This, not by his own power or the power of men, but by the power of God. God can do what we are not able to do!

In this faith, then, trusting the word of God as we commit ourselves to him, so too can we in faith and hope commit this our brother to his love and goodness, for life and its meaning are not so much questions of man but questions of God. To these great questions we can trust that God has given his answers in love and in promise.

NO FAMILY—FEW FRIENDS

When I was a young preacher, the most difficult funerals were those at which there were few in attendance. I recall my concern as to what I would do when I was first called upon to serve in such a situation. At one such funeral, the only persons in attendance were five lodge brothers of the deceased who had agreed to serve as pallbearers (I made the sixth!).

Every clergyman has had similar experiences at which attendance was limited to a few distant relatives, some co-workers, or former neighbors.

At such funerals there is no real mourning, and with so few in attendance it is difficult for the pastor to follow his usual practice when addressing a larger congregation. Often such services are limited to a brief graveside committal. Whether at a funeral home or at the graveside, while the service ought to be brief, it ought to be more than just a matter of form.

A quick prayer and a brief scripture passage may technically be enough, but they are surely not satisfying to the clergyman. He ought to most certainly feel that he is called upon to do more than simply serve as an official "Praying Sam." And while those who have come out of a sense of duty and service will appreciate the brevity, they ought to be themselves served by the Church. Their purpose in coming should be seen from its highest possibilities and interpreted to them as stemming from a respect for life out of recognition that, in faith, we are all members of one household—all children of the same Father.

The pastor will be brief, to be sure, but he will also be teacher. Those who have come have not neglected their duty, and he will not neglect his to them.

The Meditation

> And he answered them, saying, Who is my mother, or my brethren?
> And he looked round about on them which sat about him, and said, Behold my mother and my brethren!—Mark 3:33–34

We are few who are gathered here today, and we are well aware of this fact. Yet the question is not one of the small number, but one of why any have come. Our brother, so alone in this world, has none left who must be here or who ought to be here or who could be here. There are no social graces which must be met, nor customs which must be followed, none to whom we can express our condolences.

And yet we have come.

In the face of death, and in the loss of our brother, who in so many ways has lived alone and died alone, we here demonstrate that he is not alone—that no man can ever be truly separated from mankind, of which he is ever a part. Every man who has ever touched other men is always a partaker in the great episode which is the life of man upon this earth.

We have come not so much because of death, for it separates us, and holds no power to bring men together.

...me out of respect for life and for living. ...hat one of our number has died, and that ...hat life something precious and of great ...ived, however recognized, however used ...affirm, too, that this loss is the loss of

...presence, declare more. We lay claim ...same family and being brothers, one ...household of God. Thus, we become ...ed brother and recognize our kinship.

...f death, this is the miracle of life. In ...iness and separation, the family of God ...gnity of life is upheld.

...this miracle. So long as God lives and remains Father of his children, such will ever be the case for each of us, who here today affirm the household of faith and love and life.

As such, we stand in the great tradition of St. Francis, who, riding to his little secluded cave one day, met a stranger in great need. Francis was very desirous of solitude, and the stranger was fearful of this suddenly appearing figure. Thinking that Francis meant to do him some harm, he tried to hide himself. Francis, also seeking to avoid the encounter gave his horse the spurs to escape. But then the hand of God took the bridle away from him, and he rode on toward the needy one. In that ensuing meeting God met man, and neither Francis nor the stranger would ever be the same. Neither was ever to meet the other again, yet their lives were locked into one another as both were embraced of God.

The Father embraces us here and now. His family is restored and his grace abounds. Praised be the Lord!

WHEN AN OUTLINE OF THE FUNERAL IS LEFT FOR THE CLERGYMAN

What does a clergyman do when he is faced with a funeral service which the deceased has already planned and prepared for him—scripture, poetry, and personal thoughts which may reach essay proportions? The problem can be especially serious for the pastor who understands the funeral service to be something quite different from that which the deceased had in mind. I for one never on my own initiative use poetry or material other than the Scriptures, and I remain very close to the ritual of the Church. Yet from time to time I have been informed of the wishes of the deceased as to certain elements of the funeral service.

One must not handle such requests lightly or in a callous manner. Yet the clergyman who has a clear understanding of his task cannot allow even the deceased to deter him from it. Fortunately, the choice need not be an "either—or" proposition. The wise and understanding clergyman can fully cooperate (within broad limits, theological soundness, and good taste) with such declared wishes and yet remain true to his task. He can divest himself of the responsibility for use of the material by informing the congregation as to its source; but even more than this, he can use the intrusive material as a tool.

The pastor should understand that most often such requests stem either from a certain point of reference which has been invaluable to the deceased in developing a cohesive view of life and faith (and which he seeks in death to proclaim as a kind of postlude to his life and as a possible beacon to others), or from a well-ordered, disciplined, and inner-directed life, which extended to, and even planned for, death.

In either case a valuable lesson may be drawn from these motives as the pastor interprets them as such and seeks to demonstrate their general application to all as they relate to the understanding of, or the discipline and ordering of, the Christian life.

The message below is one example of this and was preached when an aged schoolteacher passed away. She was an orderly and disciplined person and had planned her funeral with the funeral director. She had left with him a packet to be delivered to the officiating clergyman. In it she had placed a poem, scripture selections, and two prayers. She also had included an explanation to the pastor as to why these were important to her.

The Meditation

> But as it is written, Eye hath not seen, nor
> ear heard, neither have entered into the heart
> of man, the things which God hath prepared
> for them that love him.—I Corinthians 2:9

Our sister had been a teacher for many years. From the witness of so many former students, we know that she was a good teacher. Teaching was more than her profession in life; it was her calling and her noble task. To prepare her young charges for life, she came to class always prepared.

The many who substituted for her when she was in ill health affirm that her lesson plan was full, complete, and always up-to-date. As a teacher she knew what she was doing, and planned and prepared so that she could do it well.

But she was more than a schoolteacher. Each of us who knew her knew that she was a disciplined, orderly person. No aspect of life escaped her or went without her hand and mind being applied to it: her family life, her social responsibilities, her church relationship.

Ever a teacher—within the classroom and without—she sought to speak her word to the world around her and concerning the world about her. She sought in this way to be fully related to the whole of life—even as it included her death.

And so it is that, true to herself, she left a "lesson plan" for this pastor which he might use as a guide in conducting this service. But in this there is even a greater lesson for us: something of the approach to life and an understanding of death. We see quite clearly a disciplined life well lived and a life so full that it included, unafraid, an understanding of death.

Our Christ, the master teacher, sought to teach us these lessons of life. In his wilderness experience, though surrounded by a barrenness filled only with a great desolation, he tuned his mind, disciplined his thinking, ordered his thoughts, and planned his actions. Though there was a vast wilderness about him, it was external to him. Within was fertile soil! He would use the fertility of his mind to make a dry earth, barren of hope, green once again in promise.

Into this world he went unafraid. Life was beautiful. Life was valuable. Men were too precious to live as anything less than beloved children of the Father. To gain such a life for his brethren was of such great import that it was worth every risk and any cost. With his eyes fixed firmly on the hope of God's promise, he went without fear to the cross. Life was so understood that death held no terror. It was a part of life. It, too, was to be found in the hand of the Father. He would know! He would care!

The Father! Yes, he's at the heart of the matter. The man of faith cannot speak of overcoming anxiety without thinking of the Christ who so trusted in God that he was able to say, "In the world you have anxiety; but be of good cheer, I have overcome the world."

Even at the hour of great peril and crying, "My God, my God, why hast thou forsaken me," he was reaching up to grasp the hand of the Father, in whom even this hour was to find its meaning. Anxiety brought to the Father gives way to love and trust. Then the order of this world is clearly seen, and the nature of this life can be truly known, and we can find peace enough to "run with patience the race that is set before us," committing ourselves in life and in death unto him.

TRAGIC DEATH

The Word of God, which is to be spoken at the hour of death, is meant to be heard. How can it be heard amidst tears and mournful cries? How can it be heard when attention is drawn away from it by the sudden realization at the start of the service that the end has come, and that soon the separation will be finalized forever with the committal of the body?

This is the question each pastor must ask himself as he prepares to speak the Word of God. When the death is sudden and tragic, there is the greater danger that the shock of that death will carry over through the service. In order to give the Word of God a chance to work its healing, it is necessary to prepare for its reception. The pastor can do this by addressing some personal remarks to the grieving family as he begins the service. This personal word, which is also the Word of God, can calm and soothe and call those to whom it is addressed to hear God's word as it comes to us through the Church.

This is a psychological necessity and is theologically sound. I do not suggest that the word of the clergyman can do what the Word of the Scriptures cannot do, but I do suggest that God can speak as well through living persons who are present as through the saints of the Scriptures.

The Meditation

> As the Father knoweth me, even so I know
> the father: and I lay down my life for the
> sheep.—John 10:15

> (Commence the service with this message
> and then proceed with the ritual of the
> Church: the Scriptures, psalms, and prayers.)

Death has come—suddenly and unexpected. We are filled with sorrow and with grief. It does not seem that this could have happened, but our tears bear witness to our loss, and we know it is true. Death has come as an invader and as a thief. It has come unannounced. We have fallen helpless before it. No time was given to us so that we might fight against it or that we might prepare for it.

We say in our hearts, "If only I could have done something!" But now, in the face of death, we know that we are helpless. There is nothing that can be done which will restore our loved one to us. Death has come, and it has separated us.

Beloved in the Lord, such feelings are genuine, and they are very real. Those who love you know this. The Church, too, understands. We share your sorrow and your grief, and our tears are mingled with yours.

The Church would not try to say anything which would ignore the fact of this sorrow. It is too real. Nor would the Church at this time ignore our grief, even as it seeks to lead us to the Lord.

The Church cannot remain silent, of course, but yet we ask what it can say or do at this hour which will assuage our grief or give us comfort in the midst of so much pain.

71

The Church is but an instrument, yet it is an instrument of our Lord, who himself knows of grief and who understands. And, as through the Church we come before our God, we know in faith that we can find a place in his heart, for he is a father who gave up a son to a tragic death.

It is out of this death that the Church was born. It was in the tears of the Father that the newly planted Church was watered. It was in the Savior who died that new life was found.

Out of this tragedy and sorrow was our Lord able to come to us and to speak with us. Death is no stranger to him. He has walked that way before, bravely and unafraid, though filled with sorrow.

And because his death is so real, we are prone to feel that he helps our dying and that we can safely commit our loved one to him in death. As for we who live, however, we wonder where we shall be able to flee for comfort.

But it was not just the fact of death that made Christ our Savior: it was that he triumphed over it! So it is that his death and his life are of one essence, and he is able to speak to us of both. Speak to us? Yes, but even more. He is able to *be* with us—in life and in death—for he is the master of both. He is thus able to help not only our dying but our living as well.

Here is One who, for love's sake, was not afraid to call himself our brother and who united his lot with us in the totality of our human condition—as we walk both in the light and in the shadow. He is with us, and assures us that when we depart he will not depart from us.

In the play *Family Portrait*, Mary Magdalene testifies to the truth that Christ was the Lord of her life and of her living. On the night of the crucifixion of Jesus, Mary is portrayed as sitting silently by a well bemoaning the loss of her Savior. As she recalls his words and his life, she sees that these are very real and that, though he be dead, yet is her life still changed and renewed. Reflecting on the realization that he is the Lord of life, she says, "I was blind, but now I see; I was deaf, now I hear—the world will never be the same because he lived."

It is from such a faith as this that the fathers of the Church drew their strength. It is this faith and this promise that spring forth from Holy Scripture—a fountain of praise from those who had themselves cried from the depths!

Hear now these words of promise and of comfort as through the Church—the prophets and the psalmist, the apostles and our Lord—God himself comes to us and speaks with us. He who believes that at the end of life is the peace of God need not only weep as he cries from the depths; he can also affirm his faith in the midst of those tears as he sings the praise of God.

And he who is able to hear the Word of God coming to him through his own lament and who can praise God need not be afraid.

THE HARD PERSON

This is a day of constant and continuous judgments. Each of us is judged on many fronts and in many ways. But at death the world seems to exert judgment in but one area: the moral-religious life of the deceased. The moral portion of that life, however, seems to take precedence over the religious aspect.

We often hear, "He may not have been a churchgoing man, Reverend, but he was a good man and will surely get to heaven." The opposite presumably is the case when, though one is active in his church and vocal in his religious concerns, he is judged to be a hypocrite.

This is especially the case with the one who is judged by many as having been sinful or evil and as having lived a hard or wasteful life. The acts become the man in the eyes of the world, and his funeral service thus presents many stumbling blocks for the pastor who would, on the one hand, uphold the intrinsic dignity and worth of man, and, on the other hand, extol the virtues of a good life which is well lived. Many a pastor has resolved this dilemma either by joining the world in judgment upon the deceased or by seeking to excuse his actions, either explaining them away or alluding to some type of "death-bed confession."

But the task of the clergyman and the purpose of the funeral service are not to do either. The clergyman is not called upon to speak for man, in either praise or judgment, but to speak the Word of God. And the funeral is not the bar of a court where a man is judged worthy or unworthy— or even where notice is taken of his worth. It is a time and place where God meets his people, once again calls them his children, and assures them of his love.

Under God we face the fact of the utter bankruptcy of all earthy judgment: "Judge not, that ye be not judged!" All of us stand under but one judgment: that of our God. His judgment, however, comes from a heart of love and stems from his desire that we should reflect this love in our lives.

Human judgments stem from many sources and evoke counterjudgments which tend not so much to correct wrongs as to multiply them. In Christ, however, while the Word of God is firm indeed, and calls evil "evil" and sin "sin," it comes to us without the sting, for we know the one who is speaking. It is he who has come to forgive and to find and to save!

The Word of God's love is a word of judgment to those who live outside of that love, and it calls them once again to share in that love. But even more than that, because he continues to call to us in love, we are assured that no matter who we are or what we have done, we are still precious to him. It is he who loves us; it is he who saves us; and it is he who gives us our value.

Let the Church say this at the hour of death, as it says this in the hour of life. Let the Church reflect the Word of God from his vantage point as loving Father. Let God and his promise be heard once again, and before him let man and his fears fall silent.

This is not to offer license for laxity and indecision. It

is just that we ought to recall that more important than our word of judgment concerning a sinful life is the knowledge that God has grieved for that life.

The Meditation

> This is my commandment, that ye love one another, as I have loved you. Greater love hath no man than this, that a man lay down his life for his friends.—John 15:12-13
> (Also, the Beatitudes may be used.)

When our Lord taught on the mountainside and spoke with the multitude, he had but one word for each of those who were gathered there. To the rich man and the poor man, the good man and the sinner, he said, "Blessed are you." To the man whose life was one of misery and to the one burdened with guilt he said, "Blessed are you." This word of grace is the same word which he speaks here now in the midst of death and sorrow. Our Christ has come to tell us, each of us, that we are loved of the Father and that the Father has freely given of himself for us.

Such a needed word for troubled hearts! Such love that we can hardly comprehend it or understand it! How is it that the Christ can so freely speak of the love of God to us when we know that our hearts have not been open to him and in our lives we have not reflected that he is Father or that we are his children?

But this is our question, not his! It is man who asks, not God! We seek to understand him from our vantage point, but he is seeking to understand us from his. And besides, he would have us see ourselves as he sees us.

We have failed; all of us. We know this, and we know

that God knows it. We feel in our hearts that this has cut us off from the Father—and it has, for such is the power of sin. But it cannot cut the Father off from us! He is and he remains the waiting Father, whose heart reaches out to us, even though we be in a far country.

One of the great saints of the Church was bent on spending his life as a prodigal in the far country. He was a troubadour of the earth, but by the grace of God, the love of God took the place of the world, and he became a troubadour of God.

One day someone accosted him, saying, "You are not handsome, your are not learned, then why does the world run after you?" He replied, "It is all the work of God. I am nothing without God."

We have sinned; all of us. We know that this sin has brought grief to us; and so it has, for sin is really destructive of all that is worthy and good. We feel in our hearts that this has also brought grief to the Father, and we are correct. But his grief has not been for his world alone, but for us who must live in the shattered world.

We are concerned about God because of our sins, and we wonder how he can forgive us and bring healing to our sick souls. But God is not concerned about himself; his desire is for us—that he should love us and bless us and that he should be our God and that we should be his people. It is he who made us and not we ourselves, and we can trust that his heart is big enough to cradle all our concerns.

It is in such a faith as this that we can find not only meaning and purpose in life, but hope also.

It is in such a faith as this that we can commit ourselves to him in life while we yet live: trusting in his love to reach out to us and to be our strength when our own strength fails and we grow weak.

As in life we can place our trust in him, believing that he knows and cares, so too at the close of life can we trust him and entrust to him those we love. We can believe that in him is life and that in his hand he holds the meaning to that life. We can believe, too, that all which he has made is precious to him and is held dear by him.

This is *his* world. We are *his* children. It is *he* who calls us. *He* is able!

Let us pray.

Eternal God, who committest to us the swift and solemn trust of life: Since we know not what a day may bring forth, but only that the hour for serving thee is always present, may we wake to the instant claims of thy holy will, not waiting for tomorrow, but yielding today. Consecrate with thy presence the way our feet may go; and the humblest work will shine, and the roughest places be made plain. Lift us above unrighteous anger and mistrust into faith and hope and love by a simple and steadfast reliance on thy sure will. In all things draw us to the mind of Christ, that thy lost image may be traced again, and that thou mayest own us as at one with him and thee. Amen.[1]

[1] From the *Ritual of The United Methodist Church.*

SUICIDE (I)

Death always comes hard. A lingering death robs those who remain of the strength they will need to deal with the loss of a loved one. A sudden death finds us unprepared. The suicide of one we love, however, is the most difficult to deal with, for amid all the emotions that are normally to be expected when one loses a loved one, there are the additional feelings of real or assumed guilt and fear for the soul of the loved one. There exists also a sense of helplessness in the face of an accomplished fact, and confusion as to why such a thing could have happened.

The pastor cannot, and ought not, play psychiatrist. His role at the time of the service is not to answer the many questions or to serve as an apologist for the act. And, of course, since many personal and private concerns are involved, he ought to be very careful that here in this public forum he avoids trespassing into the private arena of life.

It is questionable, too, whether his mention of any of the facts or related elements can help at all. To even approach this matter is to wander dangeroulsy close to subversion of his own role and invasion of the rights and privacy of both the deceased and the bereaved.

In human terms and in keeping with our concern for those who are left, these are reasons enough to refrain from using the suicide itself as the "text" for the meditation.

How man dies, when he dies, and why he dies are questions of only limited concern. When one deals with the spirit of man as child of the Father, the meaning of life, both in its inception and in its ending, is to be found in the loving Father. To learn something of man, one must learn something of God. To really see man, one must view him through the eyes of the Father.

This is what is important here. In a suicide we see man's self-destruction. So real and so vivid is this that it fixes our hearts and minds on man and on the disease of his despair. This so colors our view and so limits our ability to comprehend that we look in vain for reasonable answers which can be expected to bring solace. Man, standing alone in the valley of the shadow, can find no hope. In fixing on despair, even if one understands it, no comfort can be derived—only an intellectual comprehension.

One must look for life within the reference of life itself—God—he who will not willingly or easily aggrieve or afflict the children of men. As in life it is enough to find meaning by turning to God, so too is it also enough in such tragic circumstances to look to him. At such a time as this, there is surely the need for the Word of God to be spoken in assurance.

The Meditation

> Who shall separate us from the love of Christ? shall tribulation, or distress, or persecution, or famine, or nakedness, or peril, or sword?—Romans 8:35

God is life, and in him is life abundantly. Never has man seen him so clearly as when we see him present in the death of our Lord upon the cross. Suffering was there. Despair was there. Grief and death were there. But God was there, too!

In the life of his son, the Father rejoiced at his birth, walked with him along the way, stood with him in his time of need, and strengthened him in his hour of death. In the Christ, God showed us that he was both the God of life and the God of death, and that both were held securely in the palm of his hand.

If we believe that he loves us and has made us to have communion with himself, we ought also to believe that death is not a barrier to that love. It cannot separate us from fellowship with the Father. He knows death and he understands. Christ walked that way before, and he walked triumphantly! God has demonstrated in Christ that he is victor over death, and that in him his children do not die forever. He has made us for himself, and will reclaim us so that we may be made at one with him and he with us.

What can separate us from the love of God? If death cannot, can life? In faith we must believe that he is able to do all that he has promised. And we recall that he has said that he will be to us as a loving father.

The whole story of our faith is one of a loving God who has come crashing through time and space, through life and death, to claim his own for himself. It is the promise that he is faithful to his word and cherishes entirely his handiwork. No aspect of life and living is able to separate us from him, for while we may move to strange and unchartered shores, yet will his love reach out to us.

John Wesley discovered this one lonely day after his return home from America, where he had a disappointing experience. He was troubled, dejected, and in a state of tension. All seemed hopeless and lost for him. He had no peace and no assurance to live by. While his life had been an earnest one, he felt lost and alone and unable to provide for himself the joy of living.

Unwillingly he went to where a group of Christians had gathered in prayer, and he received what his soul needed. The words he heard affirmed: "Faith is a constant trust in the mercy of God toward us, by which we cast ourselves entirely on Christ and commit ourselves entirely to him."

When Wesley heard these words, the truth of the good news of Christ filled his heart, and he felt his heart "strangely warmed" and forever felt he could trust in God.

This, then, is the comfort of life. That though life be hard, yet in Christ is God able to press the battle and to claim the victory for us.

As we stand in tears and with empty hearts in the face of death—with loneliness and sorrow all about us—we can know that he stands here, too. And he says to us from the travail of his own life that we ought to fear not, that he has passed this way before, that he has met the adversary and has conquered.

When we hear him now, let us hear him as we have never heard him before. For his grieving heart meets ours and his word of promise finds a resting place within us.

It is the Christ who testifies now, that as God was with him in his dark hour, so too is he with us now in ours. And we can believe him, for he speaks what he knows and has experienced for certain; and his testimony—that God will in no wise cast us off or neglect us, but will come to us with peace—is true and worthy of being accepted.

We can trust ourselves to his care and to his goodness, and we can entrust this our loved one to him also. For he is both the Lord of life and the Conqueror of death: a father who is both life and love.

Jesus said: "Let not your heart be troubled: ye believe in God, believe also in me.

"In my Father's house are many mansions: if it were not so, I would have told you. . . .

"Peace I leave with you, my peace I give unto you: not as the world giveth, give I unto you. Let not your heart be troubled, neither let it be afraid."—John 14:1-2*a*, 27

SUICIDE (II)

The act of voluntarily and intentionally taking one's own life is more than self-murder. Most often, something in the heart of loved ones left behind is also killed. The grief-stricken cannot understand the despair which led to the suicide, yet because of feelings of guilt, shock, and sorrow, they suffer much of the same despair. They cannot comprehend why life seemed so hopeless to the suicide victim, yet because of the finality of the act itself, they experience much of the same feeling of hopelessness.

Just as the suicide victim himself was in great need of a healing ministry, so too do those about him now stand in need of healing grace. At such a time, the funeral meditation may very well be directed toward this need and these persons, as opposed to the meditation in the previous chapter, which was concerned with offering some spiritual assurances as related to the suicide victim.

The Meditation

> Be merciful to me, O God, be merciful to me, for in thee my soul takes refuge; in the shadow of thy wings I will take refuge, till the storms of destruction pass by.
> —Psalm 57:1 (RSV)

SUICIDE (II)

The cross is the constant companion of each of us. There comes to each of us that moment when we feel forsaken, alone and lost. Such is the life we live and the existence we share that our days are filled with many a feeling and many a need. Life comes full and it comes hard, and every moment is fraught with competing and complex emotions.

Yet in faith we know that while there are many needs, there is only one thing that is really needful, and that if we have this one thing we have the fullness of life.

Our Christ, in his moment of despair and death, was very much in need. All that he had was taken from him, his name was dishonored, his family gone, his friends lost to him, his body broken, and his life ebbing from him. He faced the end of his dreams, the destruction of his Church, and the abandonment of all he held near and dear. He was very much alone, and the cross which bore him he carried heavy in his heart.

In desolation he called his cry of despair, "My God, my God, why have you deserted me?" An honest cry, a true emotion; stark realization of what was now before him! Yet in that cry his agony was over and his loneliness ended. The Scriptures clearly indicate that at that moment, amidst despair, he won the victory and he won the battle of life.

How could it be that from such depths he could rise, while yet on the cross which carried him, to such heights? How could it be that in the midst of his clear recognition of what had befallen him he could move to stronger, firmer, higher ground?

The answers, of course, may be found in faith. In the hour of trial and from the depths into which he had been cast, he reached up and touched the Father. For in that cry of despair he coupled his need with him who could satisfy that need.

Up from the depths his cry went to God. In the midst of the fate which had befallen him, he remembered the Father, and it was this remembrance of the Father which won him the victory.

Up from the depths his heart soared, and as he reached up to God—for it was to God he cried—he could see that God was reaching down to him where he was, for the Father is not only God of the high places but of the depths, too. He is God, not only of life and hope, but God in the midst of death and hopelessness.

Of all the needs our Saviour needed at that hour, he remembered that only one thing was needful: the love of God. In grasping this, he grasped all.

Of course he had been alone, that moment when he had been forsaken. But now that was gone. It would be remembered, but no longer with power to separate or to hold captive. The words of Scripture were now more than just a promise to him, for a brief moment forsaken, but now gathered in the arms of God with great compassion.

Because he was set free, we too may be. Not so much because we are able, but because he is. He has been there before—in the depths—and he made them his own and has won the victory over them. And the Father to whom he called is our Father, and we may call to him.

Even in despair, the sound of our cry to him is our witness that we are no longer forsaken. He hears. He is with us. The victory is won. Once again, the Lord of light demonstrates that he is also the Lord of the gloom, and that where he is, there darkness flees and the day breaks forth.

We bear a heavy cross at this hour, but it has been borne before. He who carried it once offers to lift it again. He can and he will.

We need but call to him and he is there. We need but echo his cry uttered from the cross and the Father who hears will speak his word of assurance to us that we be of good courage, for he has overcome.

Prayer:

>Out of the depths I cry to thee, O Lord!
>   Lord, hear my voice!
>Let thy ears be attentive to the voice of my
>   supplications!—Psalm 130:1-2 (RSV)

UNKNOWN TO THE CLERGYMAN

Most Americans claim some church affiliation; few are active church members. The clergyman, when he is called upon to officiate at a funeral service for a person unknown to him, is often faced with what amounts to an instant biography of the deceased. Family and concerned friends seek to instruct the clergyman concerning the life and aspirations of the deceased, hoping that he will thereby better be able to officiate.

Whether the deceased is an outsider to the church or whether the pastor is new to the congregation and thus does not yet know his people, he will usually hear many times as he visits with family and friends, "Reverend, I know you do not know this man, but I can tell you. . . ." The conversation usually ends with, "Is there anything else you'd like to know about him, Reverend?"

Some pastors, too, feel that unless they know the deceased, the funeral service will be difficult for them. Thus they feel at a loss to know just how they should proceed and how to prepare the homily.

As a minister of the gospel, any pastor really knows all that there is to know of the deceased—that here is a beloved child of the Father; that he has lived as all men live and now has died as all men will die, but that his living and his dying are in the hands of God. This is what the Church sees, and essentially it is all that the Church cares about.

This does not mean that the personal life is not meaningful and relevant, nor that the Church does not respect the individuality of the person, but that the Church is no respecter of persons. All are the children of the same Father. This is the essence of the gospel.

The dedicated pastor will attentively listen to the many stories concerning the life of the deceased. This is grief therapy at its best, and it will demonstrate his concern that this life has ended. Needless to say, of course, it will help him to see and to know the deceased as a real person. Such conversation will also help the pastor to know those who are left, and will give him some clue as to how he might proceed to comfort them and to come to them in genuine service.

Except for these factors, and they are important, of course, it ought not to matter in any material way how well or how little he knew the deceased. He knows God, and he is called upon at this time to speak the Word of God in comfort, promise, and assurance.

The Meditation

> See what love the Father has given us, that we should be called children of God; and so we are. The reason why the world does not know us is that it did not know him. Beloved, we are God's children now; it does not yet appear what we shall be, but we know that when he appears we shall be like him, for we shall see him as he is.
>
> —I John 3:1-2 (RSV)

One day I put a sign on my church bulletin board which read: "God loves you . . . yes, even you!"

That evening a stranger came to the parsonage door and told me that he had seen my sign out in front of the church. He asked if it was just for church people, or for anyone who might be reading it. I assured him that this was the good news of the gospel and that Christ had proclaimed the love of God for all men.

"Even *me?*" he inquired. "Does that sign mean me?"

"Even you," I assured him.

"But you don't even know me," he insisted.

"God knows you," I replied.

He left, shaking his head in wonder and amazement.

In the brightness of the day in which we live, we can hardly comprehend what it means to know that we are loved of God. We call ourselves Christians, and yet for the most part we live as strangers in his household, in which we are counted as children.

We are not strangers to him. It is he who has made us and has called us by name. It is he who has sought us and found us when we became lost. It is he who is the Father and who welcomes us to his holy household.

Our faith teaches us that he counts us as his children and that he cannot forget or neglect any whom he has made. When anyone has been for us as much as our Father has been for us, and when we see that he willingly sacrificed himself for us, we can believe that he just simply cannot allow himself to ever be less to us than a loving father.

We can, therefore, have faith that we are able to come to him. He will not consider what we are or what we have done—only that we are his children, coming before him in need.

90

In the day that we live, we can put our trust in him. We can count on him to accept us and to receive us and to remain with us. This is the whole value and meaning of life: that God is with us.

We know this and we see this, and we continue to try to understand this very thing as we live from day to day. But hardly do we begin to comprehend when we find ourselves walking through the valley of the shadow of death. And it seems to us again that we walk alone.

When death comes, our faith is tried as never before. What we had only dimly seen we now find hard to see at all. We seek to reassure ourselves that we are not left alone to wend our way through these dark hours. But self-assurance comes hard.

At such a time as this, when life is so dark, when tears of sorrow seem to be our only companion and when comfort seems far away, our God is yet with us. He becomes the light of our life, and his word is promise to us that he has not left us and will not leave us.

He is able. His love is enough. He is the Father who will not forget any of his own. In life he comforts us with his word, and this word becomes our strength.

As with such peace and assurance we are enabled to face life unafraid, so too ought we to be enabled to face death unafraid—committing ourselves and our loved ones to him. For in death, we can be assured, he receives those we love, for they are his loved ones, too.

DEATH OF AN INFANT OR BABY

During the moment of highest joy at the birth of a child, death sometimes comes bringing the hour of greatest sadness. Hardly ever are persons so wretched and torn as at a time such as this, when they have ascended to the heights of hope only to be suddenly dashed to the depths of despair.

The grief over the loss of a child is great, to be sure, and the loss monumental in the life of parents and family. It is probably one of the most tragic of deaths, because promise is destroyed before its realization. This is so true that it can be assumed that the pastor will be careful to relate his remarks to this point, and to include these concerns in his message.

The pastor must also be aware, however, that he is not dealing with just the fact of this loss. The grief is greater in that it is complicated by the gyrations of the parental emotion which has swung from one of expectancy to one of despair.

It is this despair and the feeling of futility which are the major problems at this moment and which will keep the parents from being able to handle the normal and genuine grief which is always the companion of death.

The wise pastor will demonstrate that the Church and the Lord of the Church are not strangers to such grief and can be counted on to know, to understand, and to care.

He will accept and reflect the sense of loss and pain, and he will do this fully and tenderly. Yet having accepted this real sense of loss, he will demonstrate that despair and futility are not a part of the Christian life—because in Christ, death has been met and conquered.

He will demonstrate this, not just say it. He will do this by helping the family to see once again and to affirm what they already know and have previously rejoiced in—that "of such is the kingdom of heaven," and that in this little life they have touched a bit of God, his love and his promise; that in this little one, God has touched them, and that this touch is worth all.

The Meditation

> At the same time came the disciples unto Jesus, saying, Who is the greatest in the kingdom of heaven? And Jesus called a little child unto him, and set him in the midst of them, and said, Verily I say unto you, except ye be converted and become as little children, ye shall not enter into the kingdom of heaven. Whosoever therefore shall humble himself as this little child, the same is greatest in the kingdom of heaven. And whoso shall receive one such little child in my name receiveth me.
>
> —Matthew 18:1-5

When our God wanted companionship, he made man; but when it was necessary to save the man whom he had made, he came to him in love in the person of Jesus, an infant.

It is no mere accident that the story of God's love to

mankind commences with the birth of a child. Children are, and have always been, beloved of the Father. In calling himself Father, our God chose that title which was most descriptive of how he saw himself and how he would have us to know him.

We cannot say the word "Father" without knowing in our hearts that God is saying something about the value he places on us as his children.

To be sure that this point would not be lost on us, he gave us a most valuable lesson. When it was necessary to come to save man, God came to us as a child. Putting aside his heavenly glory, he did not count it as a loss to become a child in our midst.

When he was born, the heavenly choir sang out in joy and praise. The heavens always rejoice when a child is born! Here is new promise and new hope—creation again and anew!

And throughout the Scriptures we read of the great value which God places upon the little ones. "Unto us a child is born, unto us a son is given," sing out the majestic voices in praise.

We have just read that when Jesus was asked who was the greatest in the kingdom of heaven, he took a little child, placed him in the midst of those who asked, and the child himself became the answer of God. Jesus said, too, "Let the little children come unto me, for of such is the kingdom of heaven."

If, then, a child is so precious to our God and to our Savior, we might well ask concerning our loss at this sad hour: why such a precious one, so filled with hope and promise should die?

We are all children of the father, and in our grief

for our child we can sense something of the grief of our Father when any of his children suffer, or fail, or are lost to him. For we know that man is the risk of God—a risk worth the price of a loving father. So great is the potential of man for love and faith and companionship with God that our Lord deemed the risk worthwhile.

Though man has brought many tears to the heart of God, yet has he labored in love for his children, and labors still, because the prize is worth to him any price. Loving us, his children whom he has made, is worth all!

And as men, can we feel less concerning our children? It is hard to lose a child—we know that—but God knows it, too. He also has given up a precious child to death. As man is the risk of God, so too are our children our risk: the risk of men. And every child is well worth such a risk. To have invested our love in such a little one is well worth the whole price of our tears and sorrow. These tears attest that this little one has in so brief a moment so filled our life that it shall be forever full.

We would hope for more, of course, for the promise of new life is without limit. And so full and rich is the meaning of life that, however long be our years, when death comes, it comes with life's promise undiminished.

But this child did not live to the fullness of years, and we are unprepared for such a loss. We have come to expect that a child will weep his parents, and not the parents weep the child, so we do not know how to give up this little one whom we love.

Death has taken him—we know that—and our life will be forever marked by this loss. Yet in faith we can know that death has not erased the fact of his being with us— that we had him and did hold him in love. Our tears attest that while he is gone, he is not lost, nor is he given up.

This little one who is yours will always remain your child. You will always cherish him in your heart and he will never utterly be taken from you. The hope in which you hoped for him is real, the joy in which he was received is real, your tears are real, your broken heart is real—but God is real, too!

This is the promise of faith: that the Father who himself gave up a child to death is with us now, and has victoriously demonstrated that death cannot utterly destroy. As in love we cradle this child in our hearts, we can know that our Father cradles us in his.